Peace be with you.
Melinda Kramer

Letting Go By Holding Tight

Melinda Kramer

© 2007 by Melinda Kramer
Poetry by Katrina Kramer
Cover photography and design by
Jennifer Cook and Lauren Kramer

ISBN 13: 978-1-934666-02-9
ISBN 10:   1-934666-02-5

Published and distributed by:
High-Pitched Hum Publishing
321 15th Street North
Jacksonville Beach, Florida 32250

Contact High-Pitched Hum Publishing at
www.highpitchedhum.net

Contact the Author at
KramerLettingGo@aol.com

High-Pitched Hum
Publishing

Table of Contents

1

Author's Note

The concept of this book is to present essays that have been generated by the loss of my daughter, Katrina. Learning to process the pain is a difficult challenge, made all the more confusing by the nature of her death. It has been a journey, born of determination and requiring an enormous amount of emotional energy. I am grateful for the opportunity of growth, under the guidance of Dr. Judith Fox-Fliesser, with her expertise in psychiatry and therapy. Feeling compassion for others who are also forced to live with the loss of a loved one, it is my hope that these insights, infused with poems written by Katrina, may prove helpful in some small way.

keep your eyes ahead, mom.

but dive in to now,

swim towards the source.

backward force.

and always let your

voice

be clean and true and

you.

- katrina

Foreword

I am a psychiatrist and usually work privately and alone with a patient. By guarding against intrusions, a space is created where the patient feels safe to reveal herself in ways she cannot, perhaps even when alone.

Here we are doing something different. In the book you are about to read, Melinda Kramer reveals her private struggle to the public, including her treatment with me. Her native nobility of character allows her to share her experience so that others may benefit from it. She invited me to speak publicly along with her and I am honored to do so by writing this Foreword.

I appreciate her willingness to give me credit for the part I played in her healing. I feel like a writer or composer being asked on stage at the end of a performance to take a bow and to make a statement. This is my statement . . .

As you read this little gem of a book, you will see how Melinda grappled with her daughter's mental illness, the pain and scarring it caused, and how, with the help of therapy, she not only healed, but also grew.

As you read Melinda's story you will see that, when in the middle of intense psychic pain, it may be hard to seek help. You may think that feeling badly is deserved. You

6

may not be able to imagine that it is possible to feel relief from feeling so awful. As a psychiatrist, my job in treating someone is to say, "I see *you* in there, hold on, help is on the way." As you read this, I want you to hold in your mind for yourself or for someone who crosses your path, now or in the future, not to accept that you have to experience such hopelessness. You can feel better. Tomorrow is another day. You are not your disease.

In spite of how mental illness can result in tragedy, it can also result in heartening outcomes. As human beings can fall prey to disease, we also embody the capacity to heal, to grow, to incorporate wounds as stimuli for positive change. As Melinda's story demonstrates, even great pain can be the kernel of inspiration for generation of hope and creativity.

I hope that by showing you the warm, respectful collaboration that is an essential part of effective mental health treatment, you, the reader, will be encouraged to seek help in times of need.

Judith Fox-Fliesser, M.D. is a psychiatrist and psychoanalyst in private practice in Saint Augustine, Florida.

Pandora's Box

When you perceive yourself as capable and when a history of successes reinforces that perception as accurate, it is very difficult to relinquish control. "If you want something done right, do it yourself." Learning to delegate takes time and patience. At least, to truly delegate and not just to micromanage the person to whom you have turned over the task or the responsibility. Truly delegating means allowing the other person the freedom to assume control and being willing to accept the outcome, even if it is different from what you yourself might have accomplished. The grief I have experienced in losing a child is teaching me to relinquish control on many levels. I suspect the concept will continue to develop and grow as I refine the art of letting go by holding tight.

It is not unusual to hold tight to that which gives us comfort. We often find ourselves holding tight at our jobs, in our personal relationships, to our ideas or opinions. "I'm fine", "Not to worry", "I've got it all under control", "I can do it myself", or "I don't need help" are common refrains. After all, accepting help and giving up control brings with it a sense of inadequacy, of not being able to manage on one's own. For me, control often slipped in unnoticed, it being my nature to immediately tackle any situation with a confident and capable manner, not even aware that I was seizing control. I was not aware of my need for control, the comfort that being in control afforded me.

That is until now. This may not be the only time, but without a doubt it is the most significant time that I have had to look failure directly in the eye. Death brings you face to face with the harsh realization that you did not have control. Otherwise the outcome would most definitely have been different. If control had been mine, I would not be dealing with the loss of my precious daughter, Katrina. It simply would not have happened. "That just won't do!" When did I lose control? Did I ever really have control? Is it possible after such a life-altering event to ever believe you can have some element of control again?

It has recently become clear to me, that if there is to be any chance of feeling once again that my life has purpose and order, it can only be achieved through surrender. I must surrender the need to always be in control, tapping instead into all resources available to me. Help must be received and even sought. In delegating, it is possible to relax in the trust and confidence that capable hands will take up the challenge. Dare I say there is comfort in the realization that control was only imagined all along? Dare I suggest there is something even more powerful and satisfying than control? I discovered what that is with my Pandora's Box.

After four years of processing the death of my young daughter on my own, I came to a place in my journey of grief where I became willing to seek professional help. This is not to say that I have not benefited greatly from the help that has been offered. The support from my family and friends has kept me upright and moving forward. But, thank you very much; I am well in control now and doing just fine on my own. I am very capable, after all. Never mind that I have been developing serious tension headaches, anxiety attacks in noisy restaurants, and a nervous scratching habit. Want to know a secret? I was tired. I had become weary of shouldering such a heavy weight. It seemed I had progressed as far as possible on my own and it was time to let a professional steer the boat for a while. Perhaps a new navigator could lead me in directions I had not yet found the courage to explore. This has proven to be the case.

It was not immediate, this turning loose of control. It took some time. Reflecting back, I have to laugh at myself. We both laughed, because I was so transparent. I began my therapy with a preconceived agenda. Here are my concerns; this is what I need to work on; these are my questions; and (yes, I know it is funny) here is what I want to hear from you. Thankfully, my therapist, with her expertise, has been excellent at gently guiding my discovery, carefully introducing new tid-bits to chew on and digest, offering new ideas to nurture and explore. Seeds would be strewn; I would dutifully cultivate them all week, and then return eagerly to the gardener for direction in pruning and tending my growing garden of healing.

Then one appointment day, I found myself unprepared. There was no agenda on my plate. In truth, it had been a very busy and somewhat stressful week at work, providing me little time to contemplate my next session. Besides, I did not feel comfortable with the topic I was pondering . . . letting go, saying goodbye. Interestingly enough, there was a reassuring calmness growing as the need to orchestrate was giving way to the choice to delegate, to surrender control. A confidence was growing that it was not necessary to have everything all figured out, that my therapist and I would work together to determine what "letting go" would mean for me.

In preparing to leave the house for my morning appointment, my eye fell on a bamboo box that had belonged to my daughter. I did not know why, but I felt compelled to pick it up and take it with me. "Why are you taking that?" my husband asked. "I don't know," I replied honestly. An idea was germinating that perhaps I could identify and write down elements of my grief that are painful, put them in this box, thereby symbolically saying goodbye.

So into the session I strode, box in hand. "Tell me about this box," she requested. I rambled for a bit, still not clear about the role the box might serve, but, at the same time, both puzzled and pleased to have it with me. We tossed around the notion of using the box to house and purge disturbing aspects of my loss. An idea, by the way, that was soon abandoned. However, it did ignite a certain spark, as my therapist confided that she could not help but be reminded of Pandora's box. Although we both had to draw on rusty memories of Greek mythology, the parallel of the forbidden box was not to be missed. Pandora, the first woman on earth, was endowed with many gifts by the gods. The gifts were all talents except one, which was a box that she was expressly told not to open. Curiosity getting the better of her, Pandora opened the box, only to release all the evils of the earth. This I remembered, but there was another element of the myth that I had forgotten altogether. Therein lies my enlightenment.

When I arrived at my office later that day and was able to seize a free minute, I decided to look up the story of Pandora on the Internet to confirm what my therapist had believed to be true. Upon opening the mysterious box and being overcome with evils, Pandora quickly closed the lid just in time to preserve one thing that lay at the bottom of the box. That one thing was Hope. So this is where my daughter's box was leading me . . . to Hope! The significance was not lost on me. The only day to date that I had gone to my session without my own agenda; I had been led to Hope. Indeed, I began to realize that in my determination to hold so tightly to control, I had not left room for Hope.

So encouraged by this revelation, I jumped up immediately to fax a printed recap of the Pandora's box myth to my therapist. She had remembered correctly about the significance of Hope in the story. At the very moment that I returned to my seat, my computer indicated a new email. It was from Davin, a very important friend from whom I had not heard in a long time. He was Katrina's boyfriend at the time of her death. I had been longing to hear from him, and this unexpected and very gracious email delighted me. He was thanking me and expressing a sense of gratefulness for a new attitude he has adopted since being involved with my family and me, and I quote, "I can't help being hopeful". I pride myself in paying attention to subtleties, in appreciating every nuance and allusion that might be missed by the less observant or perceptive. This, however, was not even subtle. It was obvious.

Without even being completely aware, I had experienced the power of surrendering control. Maybe more accurately, I was beginning to feel comfortable with the idea that I had never really had control. Moreover, perhaps control was not something I needed. Without knowing the reason, I had been compelled to take my daughter's box to my session. With no agenda at all, I had been led to the notion of Pandora's box, wherein I was reminded of what is indeed more powerful and satisfying than control. The myth speaks of Hope, lying at the bottom of the box, captured there after all evils have been released. Hope, by which we can manage and handle that which seems insurmountable and which is beyond our control. Hope, making it no longer necessary to struggle for all the answers. Moreover, when I began to once again embrace this neglected notion of Hope, an immediate gift presented itself to me in the form of the email. No, this was not subtle. I got it. Now I must learn to hold tight to the comfort and reward of Hope, turning loose the frustration of trying to always be in control. Hope is an important key to letting go by holding tight.

"trails"
rocks on the shore
tempt my core
dribble in, burst free
just to touch me

each step
gliding through
the sliding waters
i will protect you

and subject you
to things you've never seen
the trickling
has made them clean

and clarifies my soul
no control is needed
or preceded
by my mind

but another kind of love
gives shelter
and strengthens my toes
like thorns on a rose

to the grains of deceit
that never cease to meet
each bubbling wave.
your sands

my hands
what peace they give
to let me live
another day

- katrina
   1-14-01

You Would Have Liked Me

Shelia had just been hired, working less than two weeks, when my entire world changed. It must have been difficult for her to adapt to a new job, working with new people, with tragedy in the air. It was very important to me not to put off going by the office after our daughter died, so that our employees would not be overly worried about us. "They will need to see us in person," I remember saying to my husband. "You do not have to say anything, and they will not know what to say either, but they will need to see us; just for a few minutes." Most of our employees have been with us for many years and would take comfort in seeing that Paul and I still looked the same, that we were "ok". But, Shelia was different. She had not known us.

Shock is an effective anesthesia. It allows you to do what must be done in times of tremendous strain. And so, in the days that followed my personal loss, I walked the walk. I can still feel the numbness, the mechanical-ness of functioning much like a zombie or a robot. Refusing to shut down, I attended to routine activities as best I could from day to day. But I was different. I was not the same. It struck me as very sad when I heard my faint voice express to Shelia one afternoon upon leaving the office, "See you tomorrow. I'm sorry, Shelia. I think you would have liked me."

That phrase and its implied sentiment have stuck with me over the years. "I think you would have liked me." Before. Before this terrible tragedy. Before I lost my daughter. Before it transformed me into this non-person. Before I became hollow. I think you would have liked me. You would have liked me because I was fun to be around. I was funny. I was thoughtful. I was capable. I was cheerful. I think you would have liked me, because I was real.

My husband and I agreed from the start that we would take a proactive approach to our healing. We would not turn away from invitations or outreaches from friends. Although sensitive to our own individual needs, we would strive to move forward hand in hand. And so, we carried on. Life seemed little more that a pretense at that point, but often when you pretend and maintain a certain behavior, it gradually becomes more natural and real. But after a time, there grew a yearning for the person I had been "before". The change in me was painful and I began to turn away from it. I wanted my normal life back. I wanted to be me again. I think you would have liked me.

Somewhere along the line, a determination surfaced to regain my old self. Loss must not be met with loss. Everyone patiently awaited my return, no one missing me more than I did myself. Sometimes it was nearly impossible to remember who I had been, but strategically I held tight to qualities that had been valued. Adopting the mantra, "cheerful and steadfast", I put forth an excellent imitation of my former self. Over the years, my performance improved, often even fooling myself. It felt good to be back! "Glad to see you are your old self again," my friends would say. Yep, time does make it all better, just like everyone had told me it would. I was cheerful and steadfast. Shelia would finally get to meet the real me.

Some people enjoy change for its own sake. Rearranging a room, replacing furniture, buying new clothes, relocating, changing their appearance, changing jobs can all be revitalizing and invigorating. Others of us thrive more fully with the reassurance and comfort of the familiar. I grew up in one house. Paul and I raised our three girls in a house only blocks away from my own childhood home. The curtains I made for our home when we first moved in were still there over twenty years later. It is difficult for me to part with a favorite outfit long after it is worn out. Why replace a cozy chair or move a desk when its placement by the window is so pleasant? My life was comfortable. It is no wonder, therefore, that with my resistance to change, I disregarded it in myself. I was fearful of the changes. I wanted to be the same. I think you would have liked me.

Recently, however, I was rereading a poem written by Katrina, the daughter I lost. The last few lines of this poem have opened my eyes in a special way.

it's so easy to be blind.
but then you miss
the preciousness of life
the intriguing difference
between peace and strife.

It occurs to me that I have been blind. Blind to the changes within me that can no longer be ignored. Blind to the ways the death of my daughter has affected and changed me. I have been blindly clinging to peace, the peace of familiarity and continuity, and carefully avoiding the strife that comes with discord and change. I am not the same person. Nor should I be. You do not lose a child without changing. You do not experience what I went through during her struggle with depression without it also having a dramatic effect on you.

Acknowledging the ways in which I am different both frightens and excites me. I am fearful, as I would be of any wound, hoping it does not limit me. Yet it is exciting to imagine that the changes may empower and strengthen me. It has been a slow process to allow that I am different and it takes courage to embrace these differences. But, I do not want to miss the preciousness of life. And, maybe now I can say in a much stronger voice as I greet Shelia at the office each morning, "I think you will like me."

I am only beginning to understand the changes I have undergone and what they might mean for my life. Painful experiences and living with loss leaves its mark in a very personal way. Just as each individual reacts to events and processes emotions differently, the resulting patina is also unique to that person. As for me, I now have a keen insight into a highly misunderstood illness, my perspective on life is rarely diluted by the mundane or trivial, I am learning that pain and joy can hold hands without dysfunction, and my faith is growing in ways that are comforting and reassuring. Peace and strife intertwine when you live each joyful day with pain in your heart, so that the intriguing difference between them becomes almost indistinguishable.

I am different, it is true, but perhaps that very difference makes it possible to recognize and appreciate the preciousness of life even more fully. I think you will like me. Now. Now that I have survived this terrible tragedy of losing my daughter. Now that it has transformed me into a stronger person. Now that I have changed in ways that I am still discovering. I think you will like me. You will like me, because I am.

"what is blue?"

what is blue?
who's to separate the hue
from any other human thing
energy
we make the lines
the times
divisions in our minds
and i'm sick of trying to decide
where i fit
that's why i sit
in such a muddled puddle
floating in the messiness
of an interrupted kiss
and my own existence

it's so easy to be blind
but then you miss
the preciousness of life
the intriguing difference
between peace and strife

- katrina

2000

Not the Mama

When someone compliments one of my three daughters, I find myself saying "Thank you," as though her talents and accomplishments are in some way a direct consequence of my own doing. You might hear me respond in a more selfless way with, "How smart of you to notice! Thank you for mentioning that to me." This said, however, with the same tremendous sense of pride, deserved for no other reason than that I am the mom.

Of course, responsible parents will also find themselves apologizing for a little faux pas slipping from the mouth of a youngster, trying to set blunders right, feeling the burden of mistakes as though they were making them themselves all over again. Parents often take on the responsibility for that which a child does, both the good as well as the bad. It is not easy to draw the line of separation, the connection between parent and child being so powerful.

Our eldest daughter brought us joy and pride throughout her life. A talented artist, a bright student, a dancer, a gentle leader, a loyal friend, an insightful spirit, her many accomplishments were far-reaching and marvelous. Then, with no warning and seemingly out of nowhere, the illness of depression seized her and within two years our daughter took her own life. The nature of this kind of loss is overwhelmingly confusing to everyone involved and the impact is fierce and disturbing. To take on the responsibility of a consequence of that magnitude is, at the very least, ill advised and self-defeating. And yet, I have come to realize that is exactly what I have done.

It is not unusual for me to take someone under my wing. Whether it is a personal friend, a neighbor, an employee at work, or a friend of one of my daughters, I am likely to offer help whenever needed and provide support, as I am able. Perhaps it is a quality that led me to teaching. Certainly it is a quality that has made me a devoted parent. But, now I am finding it to be a quality that prevents me from finding resolution and peace.

My husband tries to rein me in when I seem to drift a bit overboard. Gift giving is a good example. When I see something that reminds me of someone, chances are it will be purchased and sent to the recipient as a fun surprise. Maybe I find something that I am convinced someone else needs; then it becomes an absolute must! In a joking, but nonetheless serious maneuver, my husband delivers his familiar "not the mama" reminder. This stems from an old TV sitcom called Dinosaurs. There was a recurring scene where the baby dinosaur would be sitting in his highchair, as the poor dad tries to take care of him in his mother's absence, hitting the father over the head with a pan exclaiming, "not the mama, not the mama!" Although the intent of this scene was to represent the baby's contention that no one does it quite like mom, it has come to mean something altogether different for my husband and me.

"Not the mama" has been a cue for me to restrain from mothering where it is not needed. That, although my intentions might be good, it is not always to my best interest to assume the maternal role of caretaker. It is a gentle reminder of appropriateness and perspective. Sometimes I listen; sometimes I do not. But with the death of our daughter, I find myself needing the reminder in a completely different and most significant way.

I have been slow to realize the full extent to which I have taken on responsibility for the pain caused by my daughter's suicide. The pitfall I am referring to is different from the initial onslaught of guilt, frustration, and the sense of failure that grabs hold of anyone who loses a loved one in this way. Those feelings are indeed powerful demons to be reckoned with and may take a long time to conquer. I am describing instead a slyer culprit that sneaks up disguised as normal concern, tightening its grip until it seems impossible to shake.

It is natural, to my way of thinking, to want to ease the pain of others in the face of a significant loss. Comforting others promotes comfort and healing in return. But, my first sense of imbalance began to surface when I found myself overly worried for those people really close to my daughter. It became extremely important to me that her friends be "ok". When her old boyfriend of many years fell in love and had a baby, my excitement was considerable. He had supported my daughter during her depression and I was so relieved to know that he had been able to move on, finding happiness. My joy for him, however, was seasoned with something else.

Relief. A sense of release came over me, as though I could check him off my list of worries and responsibilities.

A new closeness has developed for the special people my daughter had befriended in the years immediately preceding her death. The unique relationships we share are very meaningful and precious to me. These wonderful young people knew my daughter and loved her. She, in turn, loved them and valued their friendships. I am so sorry for the pain that she has inadvertently caused them. I find myself feeling responsible without even realizing it. As her friends move forward with their lives, getting married, starting families, continuing with education and career goals, I am relieved.

This is a very risky inventory I maintain, checking names off a list and only then letting go of the worry. The debilitating nature of this foolhardy ownership becomes apparent to me as I agonize over the struggles of those friends who are having a hard time. I want so much for them to be happy. I need for them to be happy. My own happiness and peace is contingent on theirs. After all, it was the death of my daughter that disrupted their lives. And, because I am the parent, it is difficult for me to disengage my sense of responsibility.

Although therapy sessions have helped me to become more aware of this aspect of my grief, it will be up to me to make the necessary adjustments. It will take some time to modify. My doctor intrigued me with a conversation about how research is indicating that our brain not only stores memory data in specific locations, but also stores emotional response patterns in designated brain pathways. We likened it to the way a stream of water will etch out a path as it travels. It will take some time for me to learn to redirect my emotional stream. I want to learn.

I want to learn to enjoy my newly founded relationships in their own rights, letting them grow and flourish, unrestricted by how they connect me to my daughter. I am learning that my unyielding need to see others happy has been preventing me from achieving happiness of my own. I am trying to let go of this misguided sense of responsibility for others by holding tight to the value and preciousness of these friendships that I treasure. When I experience the stress and burden of feeling accountable for their happiness, I realign my perspective by remembering the simple phrase, "not the mama".

Starbucks and Tuna Fish

"In prosperity, our friends know us; in adversity, we know our friends." This quote by John Collins, a nineteenth century English critic, also holds true for tragedy and grief. During times of grief it will be your true friends that come forth with the help and support most needed. Caring individuals will offer assistance and lend a hand in ways that you might have never anticipated and will very much appreciate. Two such friends come specifically to my mind, both playing significant roles in my survival and healing.

How fortunate to have never been

overwhelmed or distraught throughout many years of marriage and raising three beautiful girls. This is not to say there had not been challenges or those times of stress that, as the saying goes, build character. We all had been given opportunities along the way to build character. But not until a member of our family became ill with depression, did we spin into a family-in-crisis status. With no apparent family history and no experience with this fast growing epidemic, we were not prepared for the complexity and impact such an experience would have on our entire family. I was not prepared. My world was spinning out of control and I was falling off.

It is not my intention to describe the turmoil, the confusion, the heartache, and the pain. Rather I am focusing on two needs that arose from the ordeal that would most likely be true for anyone going through a difficult time. Needs that I could not even recognize for myself at the time and yet I benefited greatly from the fulfillment provided by my discerning friends. It allows me to understand more fully ways in which I, too, might be instrumental in helping someone else in times of trouble.

Marty has been a close friend since we were in high school together. We were also college roommates. Our parents were friends before us. We have both settled back in our hometown and live close enough to see each other regularly. In many ways, we are very much alike. We love to laugh, are not afraid of tears, work hard, put family first, and communicate openly and honestly. We value that which we share in common, respect the ways in which we differ, and enjoy the fun and comfort of a long friendship. I think

Marty saved my life.

She will be surprised to hear that. She will think I am exaggerating. Marty was just being her usual self. She was being herself at a time when I could not recognize anything of myself in me. When confusion and fear blurred my thinking, worry and pain restricted my heart, and exhaustion and panic hindered my forward motion, Marty invited me to Starbucks.

I was meeting depression for the first time; it was destroying my daughter and overpowering me. Unselfishly putting her own agenda on hold, disregarding the late hour, Marty would call me with a cheerful "Meet me at Starbucks. I can be right there." Often I would oblige with a somewhat robotic obedience, slipping away from the house with a supportive nudge from my husband. Always

I would find the meeting with my friend revitalizing and renewing. I could talk, knowing she would listen without judgment. My concerns could be voiced, met with hope and encouragement. She would let me be pitiful without offering pity. Most importantly, Marty called again and again, giving me a routine that I could count on when nothing else made sense. I was lured away from my difficult situation, even if for just a brief respite, and reminded that the world was still revolving, although it seemed as though nothing was as it should be. I seemed unable to call her myself, but neither was I willing to refuse her invitation. And so, in this subtle way, during the battle, I was strengthened and fortified.

The other remarkable outreach has sustained me in dealing with, not so much the crisis, as the ongoing aftermath of the loss. The enormous outpouring of support and love at the time of Katrina's death was amazing and heartwarming. So many friends wrapped their arms around our family, giving us power and strength. It is natural, however, for the attention to subside as the task of resuming life proceeds. But the intensity of grief continues, often coming in waves, triggered by the unexpected and making you feel incredibly fragile. Again, there is a vital need for consistency. Susan is my tuna-bud.

As co-workers, we used to go regularly to a popular nearby lunch spot where we would both order tuna fish salad. It is made just the way we like it, with lots of pickle relish! Susan is made just the way I like, too. Being with her is pure joy, a laugh a minute, and yet affording an endearing serious side, as well. I always look forward to being with her and would not know what to do without her smiling countenance. Even with job changes, Susan has maintained the routine of our lunches, arranging every week for us to get together. "Is this my tuna-bud?" she always asks on the phone. Granted, some times circumstances prevent us from connecting, but nothing stands in the way of her reaching out to me. It is difficult to describe how incredibly meaningful it has been, to know that I can count on my friend to call. Not relying on me to take the initiative, she assumes the lead and cheerfully instigates our weekly time together. Not only do I get the pleasure of her company, but I also get to relax in the confidence that I have a friend who will be there for me in every sense of the word. I will not be forgotten or neglected, even when I find myself unable to seek the attention so needed.

When someone is dealing with a crisis or grief, it is certainly important to be sensitive to his or her needs and tolerance level. It is most certainly not an appropriate time to be overbearing or pushy, but often the common "let me know if there is anything I can do" leaves much to be desired. The consistent friend who offers the comfort of routine and stability by actually creating the opportunity for support is a true friend indeed. I am so grateful for my Starbucks and Tuna Fish.

The Quadratic Formula

"When will we ever use this?" my Algebra students would whine. Although the entreaty would resound almost daily, the poor under-appreciated quadratic formula never failed to elicit such a resistance. Rather than unleashing an impressive list of real world applications, I was always quick to respond with a more plausible persuasion. "It is such a good mental exercise," I would recite. "Exploring the quadratic equation will help you to develop problem solving techniques that will serve you well in any life situation." Believing the study of mathematics to possess this intrinsic value, it is no wonder that I would turn to the discipline in my grief to seek whatever insight it might provide. The quadratic formula has comforted me.

The message is both simple and profound. The insight offered is both elementary and advanced. The concept is one that has always excited me as a teacher and now seems to calm me as a seeker of answers. I have been seeking answers that are impossible to wrap my mind around. Even the questions themselves are foreign to me, as though I were being forced to learn a new language. When I lost my beautiful 21-year-old daughter at the onset of a second episode of depression, I was flooded with questions for which the answers are far beyond my reach.

That is, in fact, what mathematicians are . . . seekers of answers. Solving equations is seeking answers in the purest sense. To solve equations means, quite simply, to find values that make the equation true. That is what I need. I need something to make truth out of the unacceptable realities that I am being forced to process. A very precious member of our family is gone. How did it happen? Why did it happen? How are her two sisters, her father and I to move forward without her? There are so many unknowns.

The mysterious variable of an equation, or the unknown, represents that which makes the mathematical sentence true. It is finding that value which plagues and terrifies many algebra students. And rightfully so. Oh, not the easy ones. We are lulled into thinking how simple the process is by the easy equations. Sometimes the answers can present themselves just by plugging in a few guesses.

We even strategize with a very comfortable trial and error approach to factoring equations, stumbling upon the answers. Isn't this often the case with life's questions? We stumble upon answers by trial and error. In looking for that which brings us truth, we often test answers, discarding those that do not seem to provide adequate solutions. Excited to discover those solutions that make us comfortable and seem to work.

But just as equations can become increasingly more difficult, so do the levels of our questioning. Sometimes truth eludes us, or seems non-existent. The equation of grief seems beyond that which can be made to have answers. Coping with the loss of a loved one seems to have no solution. Yet I was determined to find some explanation that could, at the very least, make my pain more bearable. That is when it occurred to me that there is no quadratic equation that cannot be solved. Granted, a quadratic that cannot be easily factored becomes tedious and overwhelming. Therein lies the quadratic formula.

The quadratic formula is a tool, a process, a procedure, a blueprint by which any quadratic can be mastered. How amazing! Thank you, mathematicians. How satisfying. How comforting. What a relief that such a formula exists. But, my, oh my, as any algebra student would lament, what strange unnatural-looking answers it often creates. I cannot disagree. The quadratic formula often gives birth to monstrous-looking creatures with radicals and complex fractions, producing answers that shake the confidence of even the best students. Can this answer possibly be right?

The radical . . . what is that anyway? Just a symbol made up to represent a value that is unable to be written. Irrational numbers are decimals that never stop, never repeat, just keep on going, seemingly randomly, forever and ever. Incomprehensible. But, if you multiply this infinitely long decimal number by itself, a feat that is logistically impossible, it becomes a simple ordinary number. So if the unintelligible irrational number is squared, it becomes very simple and rational. How perfect is that?

So perhaps loss is similar to an irrational number. It is at once very daunting and unreal. The pain of a loss also goes on forever, non-stopping, without a recognizable pattern, forever and ever. It is not something you can write down and inspect to better understand.

How helpful it would be if we could trap our grief under a radical sign, thus giving it more simplicity and clarity. Then if we could square it, a simple recognizable value would appear.

Sometimes, however, the quadratic formula produces numbers that quite simply do not exist. A radical value might be accepted on faith, but when the formula generates a negative number under the radical sign, this simply cannot be. No real number can be multiplied by itself and produce a negative number. It cannot be done.

"Cannot be done" is unacceptable to a mathematician. The formula, remember, is intended to solve _any_ quadratic. So when presented with a number that does not exist, mathematicians simply make one up. Using no pretenses, it is even called an imaginary number. It is not real. It is called "i". And here is the beauty of it . . . if you are very brave and very persistent, you can take this odd, unseemly, made-up number; plug it back into the original equation from which it was generated, and miraculously the equation becomes true. Therein the mission is accomplished; finding a solution that makes the statement true.

So it is with my grief, with a loss that is incomprehensible and for which there seems there can be no answer. What possible solution can be found for all the puzzling, disturbing, painful, unanswerable questions? So it is, I imagine, for anyone trying to make sense out of a loss that generates a grief too overwhelming to bear. The problem appears too complicated to even begin to tackle. Perhaps the answers are much like those fashioned by the quadratic formula. They are scary, intimidating, making no sense at all. But, I submit, it is how we use these answers that is, in fact, the real key. Although the irrational or imaginary numbers cannot be grasped on their own; if plugged back into their source, truth is attained.

In our quest for answers, perhaps we must have faith that it is not so much the answers themselves that we must understand; but, rather, the belief that the solutions, as impossible to understand as they may seem, bring us back to simple truth. I know the simple truth. I love my daughter and I miss her. When I find myself struggling for more complicated answers, tangled up in the complexity of the solution, I remember the reassuring quadratic formula that can be used to solve all equations, making them true, and I am comforted.

what makes people safe?

being held
big houses, tall walls
denial
familiarity, routine
comfort
a little bit of each
some creeping sensation
that they are being
watched
cared for
protected
some set of rules to
follow
to hold in each hand
and squeeze
until its breath is yours
and there is control

knowing each sound
identifying every look
processing, categorizing
understanding
where to make things
fit
and thinking that they
always do.
hoping for reason
clinging to truth
knowing power
or at least the awareness
that it
exists.

- katrina

   7-22-01

How Many Children

The role of a teacher is changing. It is no longer critical to be a source of all knowledge on a subject, but more important to know where to find the information needed. Similarly, the brightest student may not be the one with the most accumulated facts, but tends instead to be the student well trained in research skills. So it is, I believe, with personal strength. Certainly, there is a comfortable confidence to be enjoyed when an individual can call upon an inner strength to handle difficult times, but the measure of true strength may be in the willingness to seek and accept help. It took a very routine inquiry to show me that it was time to tap into a readily available resource.

A few months after the loss of my daughter, I had an appointment with my gynecologist for an annual exam. Although I see my primary care physician yearly, as well, for many women this is not the case. Consequently, the general overall health of a female is often evaluated and addressed during the visit with her GYN. It was when the nurse was updating my chart, confirming medical history, and taking preliminary tests that the unexpected happened. It was such a simple routine question, but it completely pulled the rug out from under me and left me short of breath and speechless. "How many children do you have?"

It felt very much like a wave crashing over

me. The surge of emotion was intense and stifling. My face flushed hot, my hands went cold. My heart broke just a little bit more and the tears began to flood as though through cracks in a dam that was no longer strong enough to hold them back. Unprepared for the first occurrence of this innocent enough question, I did not know how to answer. The void was, at the time, too huge to reply with my usual response of "three" and the loss was too raw to hear myself say "two." So I just sat there with tears streaming down my face, muttering some sort of clumsy explanation.

There may be controversy regarding anti-depressants, but my GYN found no resistance from me when he suggested that I might benefit from them. I am reminded of the birth of my daughter. My husband and I had attended Lamaze classes, fully intending to avoid what we perceived as unnecessary drugs and pursue the joy of natural childbirth. Twelve hours of unsuccessful labor, dilating to a mere one centimeter, resulted ultimately in a Cesarean section and a healthy nine-pound baby. I remember after a particularly strong contraction, during which I resembled the most bizarre of sit-com comedians in labor, a concerned nurse said, "You know, this is not a contest of strength. There are alternatives." Yes, thank you, I accept.

My antidepressant does not provide climate control. Some days the sun shines; some days it still rains. However, it does raise the suffocating dark clouds high enough to provide a clearer perspective. It allows me to function more effectively without the tremendous weight of heaviness restricting me. The effect is subtle, but unmistakably helpful. It is a wise teacher who is able to admit, "I don't know, but I will find out." The student most likely to succeed is the one who can find knowledge through research. The sign of true strength is the willingness to tap into all resources for help. Now when asked, "How many children do you have?" I can answer without hesitation, "Three" and then make a personal choice whether to add "But one is no longer with us."

Tattoos, Butterflies, and a Giraffe

Admittedly not very stylish, my clothes are somewhat plain. I do not wear make up. There is a favorite emerald ring on my right hand and a personally made triple diamond on my left, sentimentally comprised of my own engagement stone, my mother's ring and the gold from my father's wedding band. My ears, not pierced until I was over forty, might be adorned with the same earrings day after day. It would seem an accurate claim that my appearance is conservative and modest. You might notice, however, that I have a tattoo.

Although small, my tattoo is in a visually

prominent place. On the upper side of my right wrist is a black circle with a script letter "K" in its center. I chose to have Katrina's initial enclosed in the circle for several reasons. The circle, with no beginning and no end, is often used to represent wholeness. I also like the way she seems to be held safely within the boundaries of this perfect mathematical symbol. My husband has a small blue infinity symbol on his left hand between his thumb and forefinger. Not only does it represent eternity, but it also reminds him of the beautiful glass figures our daughter had blown in an art class. They are colorful three-dimensional infinity symbols, representing resilience and balance. We love our tattoos!

Katrina had surprised us all with the first tattoo in our family, one she artistically designed and enjoyed the personal symbolism it represented. It, too, was a circle with two arcing lines crossing through it and three strategically placed dots. She called it her butterfly tattoo and it seemed to signify her flight toward wellness. While studying glass blowing in Australia, during what proved to be her last summer, Katrina was introduced to the popular white tattoo. Therein came the design of her second tasteful tattoo. Paul and I considered it a grand tribute to her when we spontaneously turned the car around, returned to the tattoo parlor we had just passed, and went in together to request our own special markings. My tattoo might solicit a question or comment occasionally, but always when it catches my eye, it makes me smile in memory. That is why I love my tiny little body art. And, because it is permanent.

There is a sterling silver butterfly hanging from the rearview mirror of my car. I look forward to receiving significant butterfly gifts from time to time from my daughters. They think fondly of the sister they imagine flying free and enjoy the pleasure it brings me in so remembering her. Whether it is a butterfly on a card, decorating a plate, or an ornament, the connection is never overlooked. One gift that is particularly special is a lovely pearl butterfly pin with diamond chips in the wings. Jennifer bought it for me as a special gift to wear at her wedding and it has been extremely meaningful to me on many occasions.

It is not unusual to identify some special something that begins to be associated with you. Collections can take many forms and often differ in the ways they manifest themselves. My mother loved giraffes and since her death at the early age of fifty-seven, I have enjoyed collecting them. Small trinkets, fine porcelain, and stuffed replicas all contribute in a meaningful way to my growing menagerie. I am especially proud of a giraffe I crafted myself at a glass blowing class our family took together. It may not be easily recognized, but a giraffe it is! If simple treasures can make us feel in any way closer to those missed, then what a joy they become.

My most recent acquisition to this collection is a tribute to both my mother and the daughter we lost. I have named her Grace, my mother's middle name. The name also carries with it wonderfully descriptive definitions. *American Heritage Dictionary* defines "grace" as "elegance or beauty of form, manner, motion or action." A theological meaning is "the influence or spirit of God operating in humans to regenerate or strengthen them." It can also be used as a verb, meaning "to favor or honor." She is gorgeous! She is spectacular! Grace is a fifteen-foot bronze giraffe, standing tall with her neck stretched upwards towards the heavens.

I knew immediately when we happened to be driving by the furniture/art store as she and a matching male giraffe were being uncrated, that I had to have her. Although we are regular customers and have purchased multiple pieces of furniture, I was not taken seriously upon entering the store and exclaiming in an excited tone, "I want one of those tall giraffes!" There were smaller, more practical bronze giraffes and a very impressive assortment of other beautiful new bronze animals, including elephants, lions, and orangutans. But my heart was set on the female giraffe. So with the encouragement of my very patient husband, the first purchase of the new bronze shipment was made. Grace was delivered to our yard and placed right next to the Katrina palm, provided as a memorial tree by our neighbors.

And so I remember. Whether I am gently rubbing the half-inch tattoo on my wrist, wearing a butterfly pin to a special event, or gazing at the majesty of a life-size giraffe standing next to a growing palm, I remember. And in so remembering, I smile.

It's My Party

I am throwing a party. It requires no preparation. There will be no decorations. No music. No food. No drinks. The location is not yet determined. The time does not matter. Invitations are not necessary. No one is invited. Lesley Gore sang, "It's my party and I'll cry if I want to." I am having a pity party.

It actually is not true that a pity party requires no preparation. It has taken me almost four years to prepare myself for mine. Working very hard to avert attention elsewhere, I found it much safer and less threatening to avoid turning inward. Tucked away deep inside me, tightly wrapped, boxed up, and rarely retrieved, are painful experiences that never should have happened. A mother should not watch her daughter suffer. What had always been a close loving relationship should not be reduced to a source of conflict and blame. At the vulnerable age when a young person is struggling to establish her own identity and find where she fits, a life should not hang in the balance between desperation and hope. And when debilitating illness clouds the hope beyond recognition, parents should not find their child hanging lifeless. In truth, it takes tremendous mental and emotional energy to prepare for this kind of pity party.

"It's my party and I'll cry if I want to." There have been many tears. My tears flow freely for my daughter. Tears for the brevity of her time here on earth. Tears for her freedom. Tears for those of us who will miss her every day. Tears of gratitude for the blessing of her presence. Tears of appreciation for the love and support extended. Tears for the tears, the sadness of it all. But this, finally, is my own personal pity party and these tears are for me. It has taken me a long time to fully realize how necessary they are.

Such bitter tears, I successfully avoided them. At a particularly intense session with my therapist, I unexpectedly found myself entrenched in the emotions of reliving the painful experience with my daughter. Not her death at our beach house, which, in fact, was less frightening, but rather, the disturbing onset of her illness and the swells of fear, confusion, and pain that rushed forth as it progressed. It took only a small nudge to send me plunging into the depths of painful memories. We were selling our house. The house which we had enjoyed for over twenty years, where our family had been raised, and where we had all come face to face with the evil of depression. We had moved everything out. The house was stripped bare, or so it would appear, stripped to nothing. But for me, it was stripped to everything. It was raw and so were my emotions. There is no hiding in an empty house. And so at my session, I dropped the smile and felt once again the full force of what I had been through. And I wept.

As much as I may want to minimize the effect, or disguise the pain with a cheerful countenance, or divert the attention by caring for others, the truth remains that I experienced something dreadful. The experiencing becomes a part of me. The pain of the experience has become a part of me. So I am having a pity party and I will cry if I want to. I am acknowledging my painful experience, and I cry.

My husband and I accompanied neighbors to a John Edwards appearance. I went with no particular expectations, but came away with an overwhelming feeling. It did not come from the other side, to use the phrasing of this well-known medium, but instead was generated by the large crowd that gathered in the theatre. Entering the arena, I was acutely aware that each person there was hurting in some way. Many were seeking answers, some came in support of others, but all were in need of comfort. The auditorium was thick with grief, the air heavy with longing, and the energy in the room magnetic with need. Our stories varied, but we were all drawn together in one place by a common thread of loss.

When Lesley Gore sang, "It's my party and I'll cry if I want to," she followed that line with "You would cry, too, if it happened to you." Indeed, you *should* cry, too, if it happened to you. And it is quite possible that these tears need not be shed in the solitude of a private pity party. This is not to promote the old adages that misery loves company or safety in numbers, but rather to cultivate the notion that, although individual experiences may be unique, grief and compassion act as universal equalizers. I am throwing a party. Anyone is welcome to attend.

sweet sorrow
what's gone tomorrow
don't worry about the
numbers hollow
  form
or twist
into an
easy answer
cancer as
 cells
multiplying
  dying
  and
watching the morning sheets
    rise
to meet the
  sky
watching as they
    try
and throw themselves
  to the wind
   just to be
    washed
     again.

- katrina

   1-6-02

Don't Little Girl Me

In America, directed in 2002 by Jim Sheridan and co-written by Sheridan and his two daughters, is a powerful award-winning movie. Every scene is purposeful, the acting is superb, and the storyline compellingly addresses death, loss, life and healing. It also applauds the courage and strength of a young girl, a big sister who quietly shoulders the burden of a grieving family after the loss of a child. I have known such a girl. In truth, I have known two such girls. They are my daughters.

No one likes sharing bad news. It is never

easy to tell someone you love something that you know will break his or her heart. It was late one school night when my husband and I returned from our beach house where we had discovered the loss of our oldest daughter. Noticing her car there all day, our neighbors had offered to check on her, but it was right that we should find her. It was necessary that we should find her. We were worried on the one-hour drive there, but hopeful. We were devastated on the one-hour drive back, but driven. We needed to tell her sisters.

Lauren was fifteen and Jennifer only a year and a half older. Although the two girls reacted differently at the onset, Lauren pouring out her emotions through weeping and Jennifer seeking solitude and quiet, they both rebounded with strength and purpose that continues to this day and never ceases to amaze me. It was Jennifer who knew instinctively what would be the most meaningful at the memorial service, suggesting scriptures, adding a significant poem to the bulletin, gathering beautiful pictures for a memorial table at the reception. Lauren personalized a special moment for herself by the river, tossing rose petals into the water and photographing them as they floated away. Both girls could look their grieving parents directly in the eyes and reflect the love there, even in our mutual pain.

At the cusp of heading off to college, Jennifer decided on a school in town, staying closer to home so that she might offer comfort and be comforted. Lauren pursued a tough transition to a different high school, making a decision with maturity beyond her years. Our daughters were looking ahead, making decisions about their futures that promoted positive goals at a time when the present was filled with confusion and loss. They dug in their heels, reached for our hands, accepted the help of family and friends who offered support, and slowly moved forward as a family holding tight to each other.

When given a digital art assignment to design a poster promoting a significant social issue, Jennifer produced a beautiful message about clinical depression. She incorporated a picture of Lauren leaning her head on her arms at a table, designed a computer graphic of a brain, and used a broken font to scroll throughout the page saying, "It's not your fault, it's a disease. It's not your fault, it's a disease." Besides being a striking and sensitive poster, it was a clear indication that Jennifer was not avoiding a subject that might well be difficult to confront. Although she could have chosen a multitude of social issues, she chose one that touched her personally. Another graphic project, titled "Sisters" was presented to me as a gift. It includes pictures of all three daughters and images of significant fabrics, flowers, and other scanned items that make it a very meaningful piece.

Shifting to a magnet school of the arts, Lauren was able to use her talents as a personal outlet, as well. Without the need for explanation or clarification, many of Lauren's art pieces included tribute to her sister. One is a beautiful portrait enhanced with transfers of special notes and writings that she had received from her sister. Another is a collage with her sister featured in the center, surrounded by meaningful photos and torn pictures of blown glass fragments, as though broken around her. Both girls have discovered ways of processing their loss and healing, taking their father and I along with them.

During a scene of the movie, *In America*, the older daughter lovingly agrees to provide a blood transfusion when her mom delivers her baby prematurely. When her dad asks, "Are you okay little girl?" Her gripping response is "Don't 'little girl' me. I've been carrying this family on my back for over a year, ever since Frankie died. He was my brother, too."

I suspect my daughters do not realize, although I try to tell them regularly, that they carried their dad and me on their backs. Even now they continue to lead us in directions that are astounding. As they learn life lessons, growing strong in their faiths; as they tackle each new challenge, showing evidence of determination and resolve; as they offer support and demonstrate a willingness to also receive it, they carry us in ways that are powerful and genuine.

Blind Dates

A stickler for organization, I would never arrive for an appointment without my trusty calendar. It seemed the most strategic way to keep up with three daughters' dental cleanings, ballet rehearsals, haircuts, birthday parties, piano lessons, and a multitude of other activities and events. I was partial to a three-year paper version, spiral bound with pages large enough to provide daily squares adequate for writing notes. It was advantageous to keep the calendar easily accessible and close at hand, a visual tool that served both as a reminder and a scheduling agent. Several weeks at a time would also be transcribed onto the dry-erase calendar board on the refrigerator, a helpful resource for the entire family. One date might easily slip into another, but as long as I could reference my monthly calendar, it was possible to more successfully manage a busy family agenda. Seemingly overnight, my children grew into young ladies, assuming responsibility for their own planning. There is no longer the need for my diligence and the calendar has been put aside. Now, I have lost a daughter and am often blind-sided by dates on the calendar. There are, in fact, significant dates that will not let me pass them by and, moreover, invoke fearfulness and dread at their very approach.

When asked, "What year is your birthday?" a TV comedian responded with "every year." A child counts the days until the calendar yields that one special day that brings celebration and personal attention. Always so much fun when you are young, a distinguishing mark of maturity as you grow, and a measure you hope can remain uncounted as you become older. When you have lost someone dear, his or her birthdays continue every year. Since the loss of my daughter, as much as I want to still greet her birthday with a smile and a thankful heart, sometimes this is very difficult to accomplish. I am, indeed, so grateful for the day on which she was born, but the date is now accompanied with a new sense of longing and missed opportunities. In contemplating how old she would have been, there floods a rush of images from both recall and imagination. In reflecting upon past birthday celebrations, there creeps a sense of sadness that there were simply not enough. In orchestrating a special family time to honor this singular day, there implodes a mixture of joy and pain for which it is impossible to prepare. And yet, with each birthday I continue to try, seeking a new approach that might offer some leavening.

It is a documented and well-accepted fact that holidays heighten and intensify emotions. These are not blind dates on a calendar, but rather highlighted, starred, and anticipated for weeks ahead. Beneath the surface hype and commercialism, run deep waters of family unity and personal response. Holidays touch us. They invoke desires to reach out, embracing others and provide occasions on which to feel good about ourselves, enjoying life. My father-in-law's second wife lost her first husband during the Christmas holiday and never celebrated thereafter. It always made me a little sad when she planned their annual trip or cruise, preferring travel to holiday festivities. Now I understand. It is not so much an attempt to escape, as it is a coping strategy to provide a fun distraction and a joyful focus. Although I also lost my daughter on the heels of Christmas, adding another layer to the dynamics of the holiday shadows, the time of year of the loss actually makes very little difference. Holidays are difficult. Emotions are high. Reactions are intensified. Along with the anticipation of holiday cheer, penetrates a nagging dread of overwhelming moodiness. Each year I look for new ways of letting go by holding tight as holiday seasons approach.

This new adaptation of once joyful holidays becoming undeniably bittersweet is coupled with another blind date. Fully expected is the hardship of approaching and enduring the actual date that marks the death. Knowing it will be difficult and acknowledging the appropriateness of it being difficult, does not make it less so. There is no avoiding the emotional impact this date carries with it. No degree of preparation or positive thinking allows me to escape the intensity of that simple calendar square. Although this pain of the loss is a testimony to how dearly I valued and loved my daughter, I would, nevertheless, prefer that this particular aspect of grieving be improved and minimized. It is to this end that I give credence to a very simple suggestion.

Several sessions with my therapist have addressed my growing anxiety in anticipating the arrival of one of these blind dates, as I have come to refer to them. This particular day was my daughter's birthday on which another important family event was scheduled, the college graduation of her sister. It proved to be a wonderful commencement celebration, free from strife and internal conflict. Instead, it was complete with the pride of accomplishments achieved and excitement for future success, blended with a clear reflection of her sister's loving influence and heartwarming presence. Yet my nervousness as the day drew near was evident, both by my quickness to tears and my frustration at not experiencing a lessening this year in my distress. Time does not heal all.

In an effort to console, adjust perspective, encourage, and fortify, my therapist recommended something on which I could build. In an attempt to defuse my stress-inducing apprehension about the upcoming date, she challenged me to allow for surprise. How simple is that? I was so forcing the issue of preparedness, so determined not to be unduly caught off-guard and upset, that I left no room for the element of surprise.

Granted, some surprises are hard-hitters, but I was in need of being reminded how much fun surprises can also be; like the thrill of an unexpected phone call from an old friend, the child-like giddiness of opening a surprise gift, the exhilaration of a surprise party, the blushing response to a stolen kiss, or the excitement of a blind date. Admittedly, there is the possibility that a blind date will turn out to be a dud, causing disappointment and requiring patience even to conclude the date. But there is also the exhilaration of meeting someone really special and developing a meaningful new relationship. A blind date offers the opportunity to be surprised. This new interpretation empowers my reaction to certain inevitable dates, letting go of the dread in anticipation by holding tight to the possibility of simply being surprised.

Can You Hear Me Now

Each person has his or her own vision of what awaits us after death. My faith has fluctuated throughout my life and I have had a somewhat complacent "wait and see" attitude. Each of us will, after all, find out eventually. My curiosity did not even heighten when I lost my mom, even though we were extremely close. I was too busy with my first baby, born a mere two weeks before my mom died. This new maternal instinct is not to be underestimated. Now that this daughter has left the earth, I find myself wanting to know she is at peace. It has been made clear to me in a number of unexpected ways that I am meant to know that she is at peace. Without the benefit of a direct line of communication, the messages have resembled the more common cell phone inquiry, "Can you hear me now? Can you hear me now?"

Flipping through channels one afternoon, I caught only a glimpse of Naomi Judd describing her remarkable recovery from Hepatitis C. In her determination not to accept defeat, she told her doctor "I am a spiritual being having a human experience" and insisted there was still more she wanted to accomplish. Our human experiences differ dramatically. The lessons to be learned here on earth vary from person to person and the manner in which we learn is unique for each individual. I believe our spiritual growth also varies, some of us developing a higher level of spirituality than others. I found Katrina to reflect this very special energy. She was a spiritual being whose human experience, unfortunately, took a dramatic turn and ended, to my way of thinking, much too soon. She was amazing while here and I believe her spirit, remaining strong, continues to amaze. Coincidences? Maybe. But I believe there have been subtle messages sent to establish a sense of presence. Can you hear me now?

Anticipating that our first Christmas without our family intact would be difficult, we spent the holiday in the Caymans as guests of Katrina's boyfriend, Davin, and his family. Other friends were included and going out for dinner one night, we all assembled as a large group. Aware of his talent, I began to entreat Davin to play guitar and sing for us after dinner. He would not commit and, when further prodded, continued to refuse. I persisted with my obnoxious nagging until interrupted by one of my daughters impatiently saying, "MOM!" with that leave-him-alone tone. "What?" I innocently asked one daughter. "I didn't say anything," she responded. Turning to my other daughter, "What?" I implored. "I didn't say anything either," she replied. I heard it so clearly. Not in my head, as though my manners were surfacing to tell me to back off, but from across the table. Loud and clear.

A few days after the memorial service, my daughter's best friend asked for directions to the grave location. The information was easy to relay, the most important aspect of which was to enter the cemetery at Gate 8. It was not until I was driving there myself, as I had done many times, that I realized the mistake.

Calling Michelle on her cell phone, I explained that there was no Gate 8. I don't know how I goofed with such a random number, because the last gate was the correct entrance, Gate 5. Laughing, she asked if I was aware that Katrina had always considered "5" her special number, probably because she was born on May 5. Then Michelle shared with me her own special number . . . 8.

Around that same time another special friend, accompanied by her mother, wanted to visit the grave site. I was better with my directions this time, even mentioning the caretaker's office, if they needed further assistance. My husband and I decided to meet them, but found ourselves waiting a considerable time before they arrived, visibly shaken. It seems they had stopped by the office, but no one was on duty. Instead, they found a note taped to the door, with the name "Katrina" written on the front. It was directions, which they followed, assuming I had posted them. They were led to a grave where a woman was crying. "Did you come to visit my daughter?" she asked. She knew nothing about a note with directions and her daughter's name had no similarity, but this grieving mother's young daughter had been recently murdered. It being clear that she wanted to talk, our friends stayed and listened, offering her much comfort in a time of need.

This was long before the devastating hurricane in our state gave it notoriety, and the name "Katrina" was fairly uncommon. I rarely heard or saw it anywhere, and yet the "coincidences" continued. A close family friend was drawn all the way through several departments of a store showroom to a distant escalator. Arriving, he discovered close at hand a complete bedding set displayed and showcased as the new "Katrina" line.

Meandering around in a clothing store, my husband and I both happened to select, independently, the same cute top to show our youngest daughter while she was shopping for clothes. Turns out, she had already chosen it for herself. Only when we returned the extras did we notice that it was a named style, the "Katrina" top.

These are only a few examples of what, admittedly, may be no more than coincidences. But we encountered these types of occurrences at every turn. Some could be consequences of a heightened awareness, but some have been more difficult to explain. I was using my cell phone to call a friend on his cell phone when, unexpectedly, a female voice answered. "Is this Troy?" I asked, knowing full well it was not. "No, this is Katrina." A bit nonplussed, I responded automatically with, "I was trying to reach Troy." Suddenly the cell phone went back to the ringing sound. Stunned, I removed the phone from my ear and looked at the display. "Calling Troy" it read. He never answered, I hung up, and when asked about it, he claims his phone never rang.

Recently, as mother of the bride, I was becoming somewhat frustrated at not yet finding that perfect dress to wear. Finally discovering one that seemed like it might be suitable, I took a friend with me for a second look. She really liked it and my enthusiasm for the dress began to rise. Reluctant because my daughter had not yet seen it, I decided nevertheless to purchase it. As I pulled out my wallet, my friend noticed something falling and said, "Oops, you dropped something out of your purse." I reached down and picked up an unrecognized piece of paper off the floor directly at my feet. It was blank except for the name "Katrina" written on it. We both stared at each other as the saleslady took it from me, saying, "Oh, that's not for you. It must be a hold tag for another customer." Smiling at me, my friend corrected, "No, that was definitely meant for you."

I do not deny that I am a mother missing her first-born. But, no longer fluctuating or complacent about my views, I have a new confidence in the power of the spirit. Katrina is a spiritual being who had a human experience. There still remain confusing questions about her human experience, for which I can find no answers. But, it excites me to imagine that Katrina now has all the answers. Or better yet, I choose to believe that my daughter no longer has the need for questions, in her state of pure understanding.

I still have questions as I continue with my human experience, but I am no longer complacent about the power of the spiritual being. I am listening and learning, as I move forward with the process of letting go by holding tight. "Can you hear me now?" Oh, yes, Sweetheart, loud and clear.

"whispers"

how do you want to be heard?
the loudest voice
is silent
so relent your word
and pass the choice
prevent
misunderstood
tortured
and bent
let them choose
to listen.
an unsent melody
that crushes to eternity
with your inflections
and injections
of hate
or love
too far above
what's audible.
if it pulls your drums
the inward hums
keep strumming.
quietly.
and listen,
persistently.

- katrina

2001

106

In That Moment

Guilt is a poison. Born of a wrongdoing or a transgression, I suppose it could lead to repentance and forgiveness. But when feelings of guilt spring forth from a perceived failure or a sense of helplessness, it does nothing to promote healing and, instead, seems to undermine any progress towards recovery. I have felt guilty that I could not save my daughter, guilty that I was unable to prevent her depression in the first place, piling guilt upon guilt until the toxin began to threaten my own sense of worth. How is it possible that my daughter took her own life? Why is it that

I was powerless to stop her?

These are questions that plague the survivors of a suicide; these are questions that plague *all* survivors. All of them wondering if there was something they overlooked, something they could have done to make a difference. Knowing it is futile to ponder such unanswerable questions does not diminish the asking. Wishing so strongly that the outcome could be different, every possible scenario is considered and probed. What if? What if? What if?

Entertaining alternative approaches or different courses of action never changes anything and, at the end of the day, the reality must be confronted once again and the loss accepted anew. This being true, realizing the futility over and over again, I began instead to look for ways to alleviate my questioning. It is difficult to reason away feelings that are irrational at the very source and shrouded with emotions that do not respond to logic. My intellect can often reach a manageable level of acceptance, but my heart needs constant reassurance. Rather than lengthy discourse on the nature of depression or persuasive reminders that no one is to blame, I have found reassurance in some very simple phrases.

My daughter was under the care of an extremely competent trauma psychologist. She became her patient after the first episode of depression landed my daughter in the hospital. Upon wrecking her car, she was treated for a broken ankle, a punctured lung, and severe clinical depression. This, after six months of unsuccessful appointments with a psychiatrist who was met with denial and sabotaged treatment. Thankfully, there was an awakening in the hospital and Katrina began her journey toward wellness. The onset of a second episode within two years, however, proved fatal after only two returned visits to her doctor. When discussing my daughter's reaction to the resurgence of her depression, her doctor said that for Katrina, "it was not acceptable."

It will never be known how much of her suicide was depression driven and how much can be attributed to personal motivation. That is one of the unanswerable questions. Furthermore, there is no way to know if my daughter could have returned to a state of good mental health. It would have been my preference, of course, that she might learn to manage her illness. Great strides are being made with medication and therapy, offering opportunities for successful management of mental illness, but, unfortunately, Katrina seemed ill equipped to tackle this challenge. If she was to struggle with repeated episodes of depression throughout her life, this, sadly, she found overwhelming. And so with "it is not acceptable" I find a small measure of reassurance.

There is much second-guessing after the loss of a loved one. I should have never let her out of my sight. Maybe if she had been in the confines of a treatment center. If she had only been better prepared for the possibility of a second episode. Maybe I should have done this or not done that. Did I make the right decisions? It is so easy to get tangled up in the confusion. Throughout the difficult time and even more so after, I was repeatedly encouraged by a good friend that "we make the best decisions we can based on the information we have at the time." Isn't that all we can do, after all? Seeking the advice of professionals, we had made careful, informed decisions. Throughout life, some decisions prove to be positive and some become mistakes from which we learn. Decisions are always choice, and so, with this reminder, that "we make the best decisions we can based on the information we have at the time," I find more reassurance.

Feelings of inadequacy or helplessness can sometimes be waylaid by coming to terms with "uncontrollability". That is quite a word, but it speaks to gaining an understanding of that for which there is no control. My therapist suggested that depression and the outcomes of those suffering from the illness are ultimately beyond our control. This did not sit well with me. Granted, I do not relinquish control, or at least the elusion of control, easily. But here was a professional whose very career implies a desire to, if not control, at the very least, positively influence the successful recovery or management of mental illness, professing to have no control. When I challenged my therapist with this apparent contradiction, she qualified her comment and elaborated in such a way as to provide me with what would become my strongest phrase of reassurance.

The doctor explained that when she works with a patient, it is, of course, her hope that "in that moment" she can be effective and helpful, but that when the patient leaves the office, her influence has extended beyond her control. "In that moment." These are the three words to which I surrender my feelings of guilt and helplessness. I did the best I could in the moments afforded me. A moment is so small. A moment can be monumental. Looking back, hoping for some sort of sign or clue, I inspected and scrutinized each moment one by one until, exhausted and emotionally drained, I would return once again to the facts as I know them. My helplessness or influence was only as effective as it could be "in that moment". Only my daughter was there all the time. Only she could take true ownership of her illness, her choices, and her life. There is much reassurance in the knowledge that I did the best I could "in that moment." And more importantly, bless her heart, maybe, just maybe, so did my daughter.

"celebration"

being pulled to a new
  side of things
lulled into a clear tide of
  peace.
however brief.
  twisted
by an easy race to leave
and hurried so that we forget
  to see.
what's now.

  so stay
until you think you're free-
listening to the glass come clean.
  let's laugh until
  our eyes both
    leak,

jump between the air

we need –

and breathe . . .

as though we've reached the

height of what's to come.

breathe . . .

as though you've realized

that you are a poem.

breathe . . .

this opening taste of

celebration.

- katrina
11-11-02

Parallel Lines

Teaching high school math immediately after graduating from college, it did not take long to realize a Masters degree would be beneficial. Fortunately, I was young and single, so did not mind the strenuous pace of teaching all day and attending graduate school at night. Most of the classes soon blurred into an MAT degree and an increased pay scale, but the impact of one course in particular has stuck with me. The course was a non-Euclidean geometry course, in which we explored the concept of parallel lines intersecting.

Euclid was a Greek mathematician who developed many of the principles on which we base our geometric models. Euclidean Geometry is the course many students take in high school. Given a few basic axioms, accepted without proof, an entire mathematical system can be devised. A man of the field, Henri Poincare, said, "One geometry cannot be more true than the other; it can only be more convenient." Non-Euclidean geometry is not so convenient and can, in fact, be very confusing. I vividly remember the grueling proofs that demanded multiple days of class time and, filling the chalkboard completely each day, required pages upon pages of notes. This elliptical geometry that we studied treats straight lines as great circles on the surface of a sphere. In order to understand the resulting theorems this generated, it was necessary to completely disregard the familiar concepts of geometry that I had studied up to that point. One such concept is parallel lines.

In Euclidean geometry parallel lines never cross, never intersect; never have even one point in common, although they extend forever and ever. But in this new model, parallel lines do intersect. They intersect at infinity. Moreover, parallel lines, extending indefinitely in either direction, intersect in one direction at positive infinity and in the opposite direction at negative infinity and these two infinities are the same point. This concept was difficult to wrap my mind around then and still intrigues me all these many years later.

It is not easy to grasp a notion when it goes against everything you have previously understood and accepted as true. So it is when you lose someone you hold dear. It shakes the very foundation on which you have built your life. Especially when the loss is untimely or seems to defy the natural order of things. The loss of a child is such an enigma, throwing a parent into a completely unfamiliar realm. It is in this foreign mindset that I revisited my experience with non-Euclidean geometry.

My children have always teased me about my enthusiasm for math. All three being incredibly talented artists, they do not share my excitement about factoring, limits, irrational numbers, derivatives, circles and parallel lines. "Oh no, here she goes again," they might murmur at the dinner table, glancing at each other with sympathetic grins. This, while I spin off on some mathematical tangent (another great concept, by the way) suggested by some perfectly innocent remark. "Isn't it amazing?" I would pose. "If you cut the distance in half, then cut the remaining distance in half again and keep doing this forever and ever, you will get incredibly close, but never actually reach the goal. Never!"

Parallel lines are so beautiful. They extend perfectly aligned. Forever. Never stopping. Always side by side, as if supporting each other. The slightest veering off course would make them eventually collide, their intersection a violation of the very definition of parallel. The integrity of parallel lines is comforting. The consistent imagery of parallels is orderly and peaceful. Parallels are pleasing. Perhaps when lives are in harmony with others, we are like parallel lines, running along side each other in perfect alignment.

These lives, like parallels, complement each other, adding depth and beauty. A line all by itself can be ordinary, as would a life lived in isolation. A line intersected by an array of crossing lines can appear chaotic and cluttered, as would a life scored with conflict and opposition. But when parallels line up, there is richness to the plane, as those with whom we align ourselves make our lives rich.

So what about this notion of redefining parallels? It throws a real curve into Euclid's fifth postulate. And yet, what a great concept! Corresponding points of parallel lines are still equidistant from each other and parallel lines still extend forever to infinity. But now we are to imagine that they all intersect in exactly one point when they reach infinity.

This new idea is difficult to picture in a concrete way. My understanding of parallels makes it seem contradictory to imagine that point at which they meet. But, I relish the notion. I look forward to a clearer perception when the parallel lines of the important people in my life, those whom I love and value, those who may have traversed the parallel faster or slower than I, all reach infinity and finally meet at one point. For there, where parallel lines intersect, we will all be together again.

Dog Gone

The phone call was unexpected, the news was a huge surprise, and the negative reaction was unmistakable. In fact, we were all less than thrilled to hear Katrina, living at home during this time, share her excitement about being given a dog. She had acquired a young, female mixed breed with a need to chase anything that moved, the ability to leap tall fences, and the speed to outrun even the most determined pursuer. Nevertheless, concessions were made, compromises were established, and this sweet, beautiful dog soon won all our hearts. More importantly,

Kaya became, in every sense of the word, my daughter's best friend. Although limiting the choices when moving into an apartment of her own and adding challenges to activities and travels, Katrina and her dog were inseparable. Kaya was with my daughter when she took her last breath.

Having just lost one of her own two dogs, it was mutually beneficial when my daughter's close friend, Michelle, welcomed Kaya into her family. It was very gratifying to observe this special dog thriving on the love and nurturing she received in her new home. The emotions stirred in me during occasional visits were typically a mixture of gratitude and nostalgia, but always accompanied by a strong feeling of connection. Looking into the eyes of the dog she had loved always filled me with a sense of closeness to my daughter.

As is unavoidable with life, time passes, things change, people move away, and consequently my visits with Kaya became less frequent. During the most recent opportunity to be together, after more than a two-year interim, my reaction upon seeing her was disconcerting. Only during an enlightening discussion with my therapist did the full significance of my response become clear. Although initially disturbing, in retrospect, my unusual reaction represents a crucial element of processing grief. Kaya has made an extremely significant contribution to my understanding and acceptance of the loss of my daughter.

Simply put, I was taken aback by the physical appearance of this older, heavier dog when she greeted us. Kaya did not look as expected. She did not look as remembered and it made me sad. Both surprised and perplexed by my emotional reaction, there was, nevertheless, no denying it. Surely it was natural in this amount of time for an animal to exhibit signs of aging. Perhaps, my melancholy mood was brought on by this visual reminder that youth gives way to old age. Yet I suspected it was more than this, made apparent by my unwittingly focusing so intently on Kaya. It seemed I was searching for something, longing for something, and left to feel frustrated and disappointed when I could not find it. What was I seeking? What was missing?

Yet another disappointing observation regarding Kaya occurred during this same visit. In an art sketchbook belonging to my daughter, I had discovered a page on which she had written a poem and then painted a wonderful watercolor of her dog directly over it. Having it framed, I had given this treasure to Michelle as a gift and was now sorry to notice that the sunlight had taken its toll on the artwork. The watercolor of Kaya had almost completely faded away, leaving merely a hint of the figure still visible. Perhaps this speaks more accurately of my low spirits upon seeing Kaya and sensing that something was missing.

More specifically, I was disheartened to discover the connection this dog had always elicited from me for my daughter was fading away. Previously, looking at Kaya, hundreds of mental pictures would flash through my mind, conjuring up an authentic sense of Katrina. They would be romping, laughing, playing, living, loving, teasing, comforting, trusting, and enjoying each other. Now for the first time this enchantment was not occurring. Kaya had changed and when I looked at her, I saw only Kaya. I beheld a beautiful, strong, albeit older, dog that was growing and evolving. Clinging so desperately to my memories and the joyful feelings Kaya had always evoked, I very much wanted her original appearance to be preserved.

This is, of course, not possible and, moreover, would prove counterproductive to moving forward. Kaya will always possess a special bond to my daughter. My inability to enjoy that connection and appreciate the added richness of her years thereafter seems more an indication of my own limitations and stunted progress.

So it is with my loss and grief. Perhaps as a necessity for survival, or possibly indicative of my own particular coping style, I had been devoting enormous amounts of energy to successfully keeping my grief totally contained. In this way my pain was manageable. For a while, managing sorrow is enough. Managing loss is far preferred over being disabled by it. After a time, however, this restrictive approach of containment becomes stifling and there is the need for growth. Life demands growth, after all. It has taken time, patience, and hard work, but thankfully, I am finally releasing my pain and loss from the confines of suppression and learning instead to integrate my grief into all aspects of living. In letting go by holding tight, I am allowing for growth.

"i am peaceful"

sometimes i think
about yellow corn
and fan blades and
hot glass. and i'm
dancing to weezer
with five different
scarves twirling
behind me. i
agree to meet kaya
in the service road
lawn, eating nothing
but butterflies
and biscuits all
the way to nirvana.
and sometimes i sleep
naked and go
swimming at
night in the
sprinklers and
the ocean. most
of the time i
think of love,
and i am peaceful.

- katrina
5-30-02